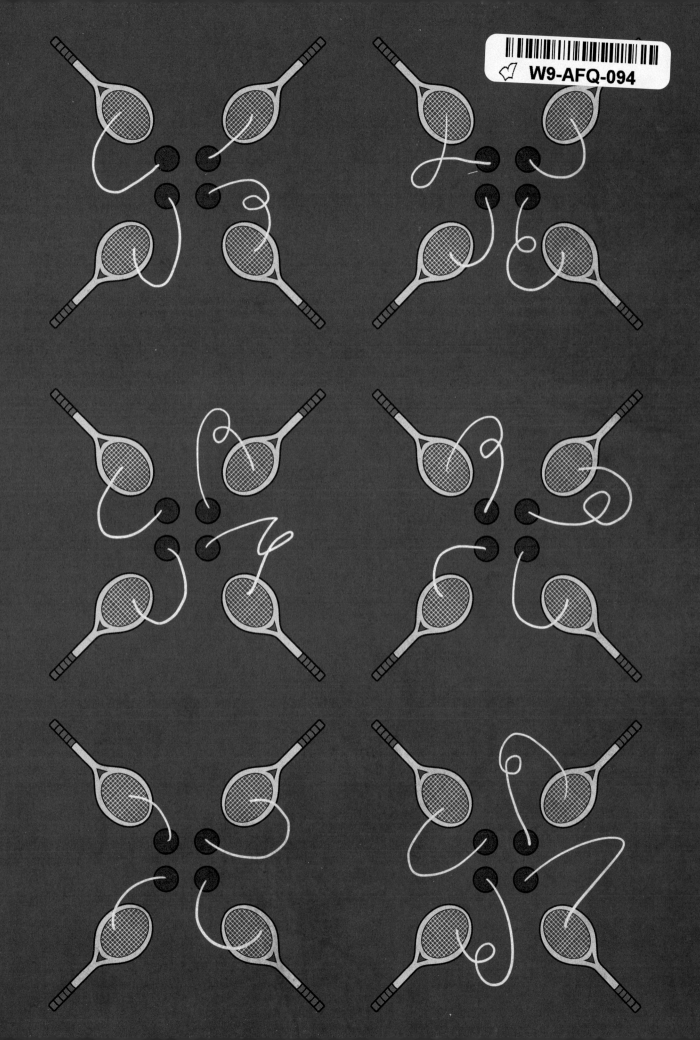

A shout-out to all the strong female warriors—
Melanie Grimes, this one's for you! —*Michelle Lord*

Maria's story is true for so many of us. . . . I dedicate this book
to all the little Pakistani girls who dream big.
I hope they go against the grain and follow their hearts!
—*Shehzil Malik*

STERLING CHILDREN'S BOOKS
New York

An Imprint of Sterling Publishing Co., Inc.
1166 Avenue of the Americas
New York, NY 10036

ISBN 978-1-4549-3136-2

Distributed in Canada by Sterling Publishing Co., Inc.
c/o Canadian Manda Group, 664 Annette Street
Toronto, Ontario M6S 2C8, Canada
Distributed in the United Kingdom by GMC Distribution Services
Castle Place, 166 High Street, Lewes, East Sussex BN7 1XU, England
Distributed in Australia by NewSouth Books
University of New South Wales, Sydney, NSW 2052, Australia

For information about custom editions, special sales, and premium and corporate purchases, please contact
Sterling Special Sales at 800-805-5489 or specialsales@sterlingpublishing.com.

Manufactured in China

Lot #:
2 4 6 8 10 9 7 5 3 1
05/19

sterlingpublishing.com

Cover and interior design by Irene Vandervoort

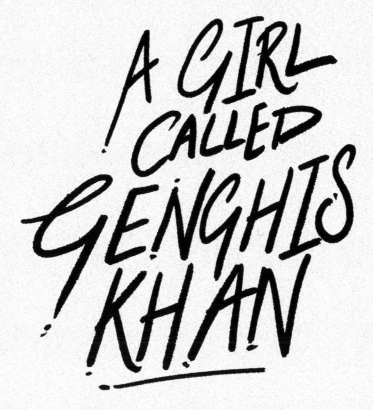

A GIRL CALLED GENGHIS KHAN

How MARIA TOORPAKAI WAZIR Pretended to Be a Boy,
Defied the Taliban, and Became a World Famous Squash Player

MICHELLE LORD

illustrated by SHEHZIL MALIK

STERLING CHILDREN'S BOOKS
New York

Not long ago among the rugged hills of Pakistan, there lived an equally rugged girl named Maria.

Sweeping the packed mud floor, four-year-old Maria watched her brother kick a ball back and forth with friends. Her feet itched to dash after them. But Pashtun tribal culture demanded that women and girls stay indoors. Moor (Mother) taught Maria to flatten blobs of dough with her palm to make naan. Maria yawned. She longed for the fresh air, the sunshine, and the outdoor games boys enjoyed.

Sometimes, Baba (Father) gave in, allowing Maria to roam outside. One day, she came upon a group of men playing volleyball. She hovered nearby. When the ball bounced toward her, she spiked it.

A man growled at her. "Go away!"
When he saw that she was a girl, he slapped her face.
Her small hands curled into fists.

Soon after, Maria chopped off her hair,
cast her dresses into the fire,
and borrowed her brother's pants.
When Baba called her Genghis Khan after the
great warrior, she beamed.
Maria's parents believed in equal rights and
supported her dreams—it didn't matter if such
dreams were forbidden.

As Genghis, Maria felt free.
She raced down the street.
She tussled with boys.
She hunted with her brothers.
None of the villagers realized that this rough-and-
tumble boy was Maria.

All the while, Maria and her family feared the Taliban. This violent group demanded women not be seen or heard in public. No education for girls. No books. No television. Sports were forbidden—and still are.

IN PUBLIC, WOMEN MUST BE COVERED HEAD-TO-TOE IN A BURQA

WITH ONLY A MESH COVERING IN FRONT TO SEE THROUGH.

THEY MUST NOT WEAR SHOES THAT MAKE NOISE WHILE THEY WALK.

Maria's family moved to the city of Peshawar when she
was ten and introduced her as their son Genghis.
No one questioned it.

As Genghis, Maria spent her days brawling, bickering, and battling—whatever the challenge, she wanted to win. Wrestling boy after boy, she often came home scratched and bruised. Baba worried. He encouraged his daughter to direct her wildness into sports.

Twelve-year-old Genghis watched athletes dart and dive in the glass-walled squash court. She yearned to try. She pushed up her sleeves and grabbed a ball. Swinging her racquet, she served.

WA-POW. WHOOSH. WHACK.

The rubber ball ricocheted off the walls before hitting the floor. Genghis hopped from foot to foot. *Right, left. right, left, right.* Adrenaline surged.

Sweat trickled.

Her opponent smacked the ball, and they rallied, taking turns.

Then Genghis smashed a volley shot, and her challenger failed to keep the ball inside the lines.

"Out!"

Genghis scored another point to win the match 9-0.

She threw her hands into the air—victory.

ONCE I BEGAN PLAYING SPORTS, MY ENERGY WAS CHANNELLED IN A POSITIVE WAY.

Rather than hitting people, I started hitting squash balls!

SCORE!

Genghis was hooked! But the club she wanted to join required official players to submit a birth certificate to enroll. Her stomach churned. Everyone would discover that Genghis was actually a girl named Maria. Her cheeks flushed the color of saffron threads. Would the director of the club tell her to go away? Was she good enough? Would the Taliban find out and punish her?

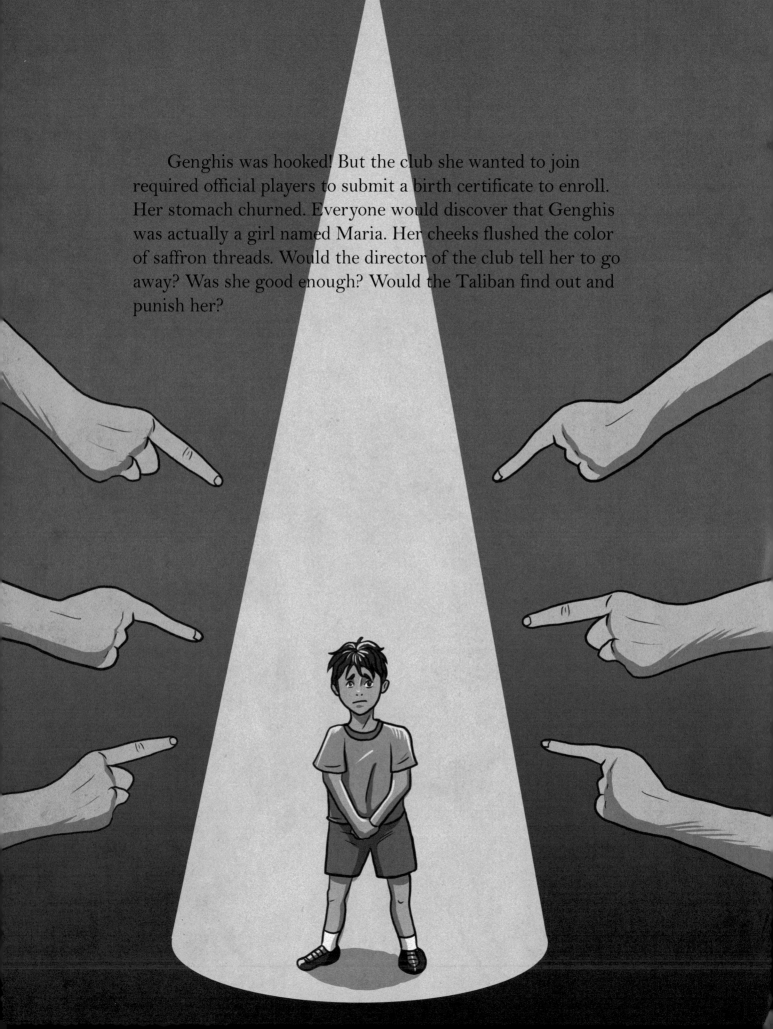

Genghis held her breath as Baba presented a birth certificate.
It seemed like
FOREVER . . .
The director studied it.
He stared at the child in front of him . . .

She gasped when the director presented a racquet and
said, "Welcome."
She was the only girl among four hundred boys.
Swallowing her fear, she clutched the handle.

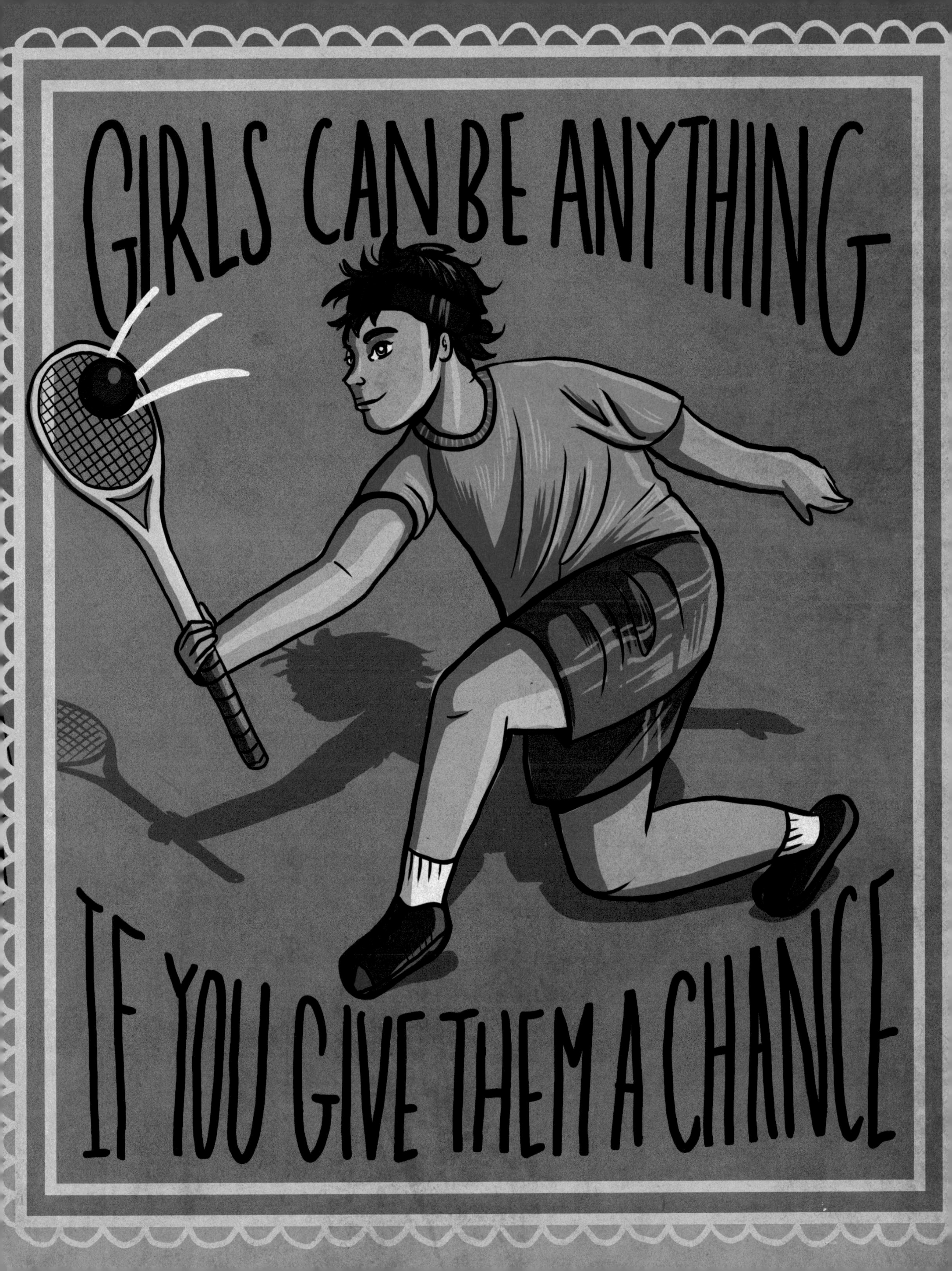
GIRLS CAN BE ANYTHING
IF YOU GIVE THEM A CHANCE

With Maria's secret out, classmates bullied her.
Townspeople battered her. Teammates called her names,
especially when she outplayed them. They wanted her to
go away . . .

When I was a guy, nobody cared—everyone was happy.
When I became a girl, everything

I HAD TO FIGHT TO PLAY,
FIGHT FOR MY BELIEFS
FIGHT FOR THE RIGHT
TO JUST—
BE WHO I

Still Maria held her head high like a warrior and practiced until her hands turned black and blue. *WA-POW. WHOOSH. WHACK.* She won match after match.

When Maria received an award from the president of Pakistan for outstanding achievement, the Taliban threatened her squash club, her family, and her life.

She heard her heartbeat pounding in her ears. Baba spoke in whispers. Moor hugged her children tight. Maria practiced in secret, and only in the middle of the night—on a rickety, abandoned court.

EVERY DAY MY FAMILY IS RISKING [EVERYTHING FOR ME].

Maria feared the Taliban would hurt her family and the other players in her club. With a heavy heart, she quit the club, but she wouldn't quit the game. She pretended her bedroom was a squash court.

For ten hours a day,
365 days a year,
for more than *three years*,
she struck a ball against the concrete walls of her bedroom.

In every moment, Maria dreamt of becoming a world champion.

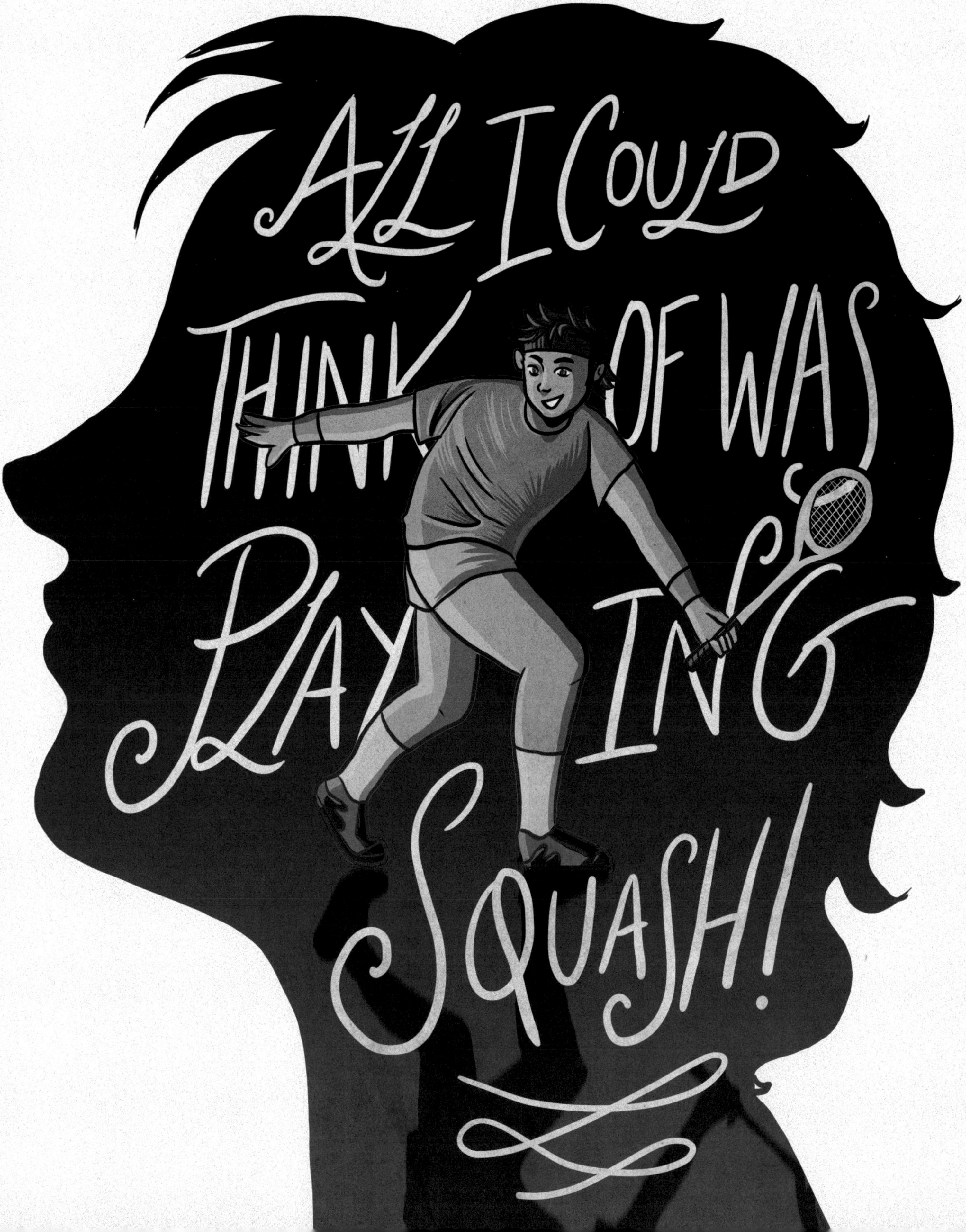
ALL I COULD THINK OF WAS PLAYING SQUASH!

Maria lost track of the days, her body ached, and she felt hollow inside. She knew she had to do something.

She emailed thousands of squash clubs around the world, asking for help. Maybe one of them would sponsor her so she could play in freedom—far from the reach of the Taliban.

She waited
day
after day
after day . . .

Finally, Maria received a message. As she read it, her heartbeat bounced around her chest like a squash ball around a court. Former world champion Jonathan Power offered to train her in Canada! Still, her throat tightened and her hands trembled. Could she leave everything she knew to chase a dream?

Pakistan is the country where I was born. I love that country, and it's like a mother.

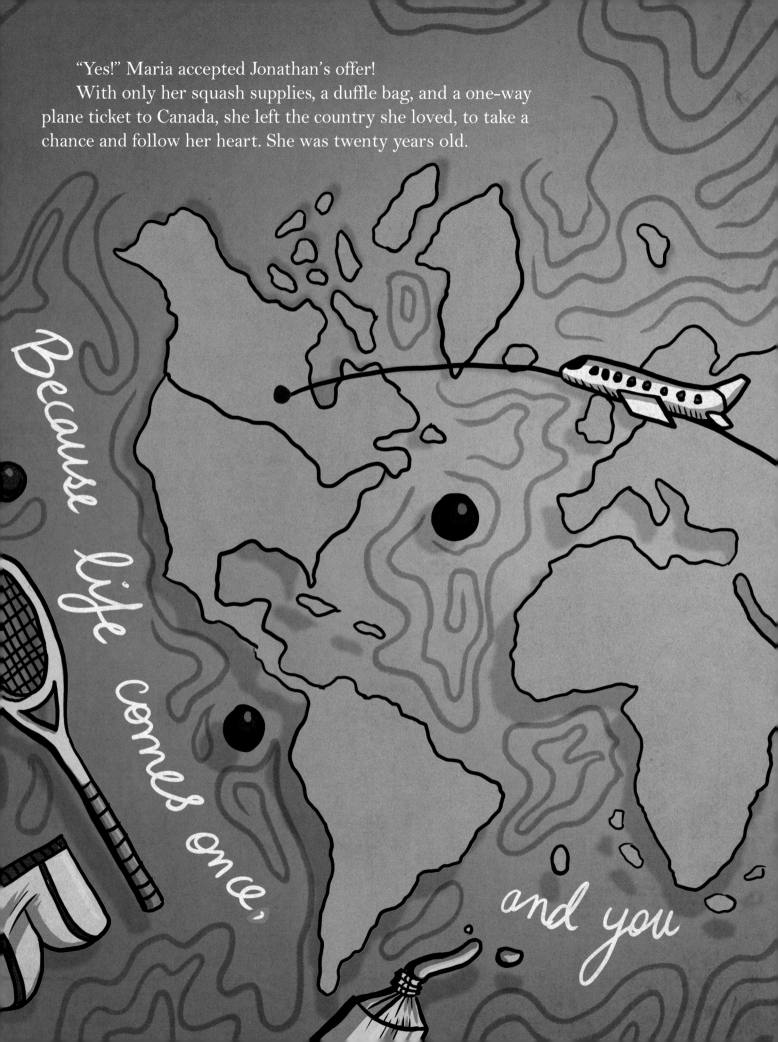

"Yes!" Maria accepted Jonathan's offer!
    With only her squash supplies, a duffle bag, and a one-way plane ticket to Canada, she left the country she loved, to take a chance and follow her heart. She was twenty years old.

Because life comes once,

and you

In Toronto, Maria trained with Jonathan twice a day at the National Squash Academy. She learned to play guitar, rode the subway, and ate her first cheeseburger. But she also honored her traditions by praying five times a day, talking to her family each weekend, and representing Pakistan in tournaments.

Maria focused on her body and her mind.
She stretched,
        she sprinted,
                and she studied.

She puffed,
        she panted,
                and she planned.

WA-POW. WHOOSH. WHACK. Maria worked to become the number one female playing for Pakistan and one of the top fifty women players in the world. She never let the Taliban destroy her love of sports.

I am a WARRIOR,
I was born a WARRIOR,
I will die like a WARRIOR.

Today, among the rugged hills of Pakistan, girls dream of equality . . . Always the warrior, Maria fights to give them a chance to live their fullest lives. She is building health clinics, schools, and sports centers for girls *AND* boys.

I feel that this is my responsibility. I HAVE TO RAISE MY VOICE FOR THE OTHER GIRLS... I THINK CHANGE WILL COME. *It will come, definitely.*

AFTERWORD

Born on November 22, 1990, Maria Toorpakai Wazir grew up among the jagged mountains of Pakistan. This region is known as the Tribal Areas. The laws of Pakistan do not apply here. Instead, elders and religious leaders govern the tribes according to the traditions of their ancestors. Women stay inside the house with few freedoms. "The more sons you have, the . . . stronger your family is, and no one wants a daughter," said Maria. Luckily, Maria's parents had different beliefs, and they gave their sons *and* daughters equal support and access to opportunities.

In 2001, the Taliban took control of Maria's homeland. They banned education for girls, bombing more than 160 schools. The Taliban demanded women cover themselves from head to toe with heavy cloth burqas. They beat women for dancing, riding bicycles, or playing sports. They didn't allow men to shave. President Obama once called the Tribal Areas "the most dangerous place in the world." The cities in Pakistan were not as strict or dangerous as the Tribal Areas, but for a young woman who wanted to play sports, it was hard to find support even there.

Maria learned bravery from her mother, who was the only girl in her village to go to school and who went on to teach other girls despite threats from the Taliban. Maria learned moxie from her father, who wanted equality and education for his sons *and* daughters. He was punished for his beliefs and called crazy, but he encouraged Maria to follow her dreams—even when his daughter dressed as a boy so she could run free and play sports. Maria says he was "like a shield" who protected her and her sister. It turns out Baba had *two* extraordinary daughters: Maria's sister is currently the youngest member of parliament in Pakistan!

Squash is a beloved sport in Pakistan. Some girls and women play in the more progressive areas of the country, but never in the areas controlled by the Taliban where Maria came from.

At twenty years old, Maria moved to Canada. She visited her homeland in 2014. She taught boys and girls squash to show that anyone could play. She also donated food, clothing, and shoes to those in need, and she is building a much-needed hospital. For Maria, her work serves God and is a vital part of her Muslim faith.

Maria moved back to Pakistan in January 2017 and continues to play squash even though the Taliban still threatens her. The Maria Toorpakai Foundation is changing the lives of girls through education and sports. She has also been appointed to the International Olympic Committee's Women in Sport Commission to help promote the rights and well-being of women and girls in sport.

ADDITIONAL READING ABOUT OTHER INSPIRATIONAL WOMEN

Copeland, Misty. Illustrated by Christopher Myers. *Firebird*. New York: G.P. Putnam's Sons Books for Young Readers, 2014

Engle, Margarita. Illustrated by Rafael López. *Drum Dream Girl: How One Girl's Courage Changed Music*. Boston: HMH Books for Young Readers, 2015

Gray, Karlin. Illustrated by Christine Davenier. *Nadia: The Girl Who Couldn't Sit Still*. Boston: HMH Books for Young Readers, 2016

Hood, Susan. *Shaking Things Up: 14 Young Women Who Changed the World*. New York: HarperCollins, 2018

Ignotofsky, Rachel. *Women in Sports: 50 Fearless Athletes Who Played to Win*. California: Ten Speed Press, 2017

Zietlow Miller, Pat. Illustrated by Frank Morrison. *The Quickest Kid in Clarksville*. San Francisco: Chronicle Books, 2016

L.S. Patrick, Jean. Illustrated by Adam Gustavson. *Long-Armed Ludy and the First Women's Olympics*. Massachusetts: Charlesbridge, 2017

Peoples-Riley, Daria. *This Is It*. New York: Greenwillow Books, 2018

Skeers, Linda. Illustrated by Livi Gosling. *Women Who Dared: 52 Stories of Fearless Daredevils, Adventurers, and Rebels*. Illinois: Sourcebooks Jabberwocky, 2017

Stauffacher, Sue. Illustrated by Greg Couch. *Nothing but Trouble: The Story of Althea Gibson*. Iowa: Dragonfly Books; Reprint edition, 2011

Lynn Williams, Karen. Illustrated by Doug Chayka. *Four Feet, Two Sandals*. Michigan: Eerdmans, 2007

Wallmark, Laurie. Illustrated by Katy Wu. *Grace Hopper: Queen of Computer Code*. New York: Sterling Children's Books, 2017

Winter, Jeanette. *Malala, a Brave Girl from Pakistan/Iqbal, a Brave Boy from Pakistan: Two Stories of Bravery*. California: Beach Lane Books, 2014

Yousafzai, Malala. Illustrated by Kerascoët. *Malala's Magic Pencil*. New York: Little, Brown Books for Young Readers, 2017

SELECTED BIBLIOGRAPHY

Bhuyan, Pretty. "Interview: Pakistani Squash Star Maria Toorpakai Wins Victories On- and Off-Court." *Asia Society*. N.p., 7 June 2016. Web. 26 July 2016.

"Catalyst for Change - Maria Toor Pakay." *TSN*. The Sports Network, 2011. Web. 9 Aug. 2016.

Jinkinson, Bethan. "Maria Toorpakai: The Pakistani Squash Star Who Had to Pretend to Be a Boy." *BBC News*. BBC World Service, 2 Mar. 2016.

Katz, Brigit. "Meet the Pakistani Squash Champion Who Disguised Herself as a Boy." *Women in the World in Association with The New York Times WITW*. NYTimes, 08 Apr. 2016.

Montague, James. "Squash Star Takes on the Taliban: 'Chosen One' Fights for a Cause." *CNN*. Cable News Network, 19 Feb. 2013.

"Pakistani Female Squash Player Rallies on." *Al Jazeera English*. N.p., 24 Dec. 2012.

Quick, David. "Young Pakistani Woman Who Defied Taliban to Play Squash Talks in Charleston." *Post and Courier*. N.p., 11 Nov. 2014.

Toorpakai-Wazir, Maria. "Squashing Extremism." TEDxTeen. Mar. 2013. Lecture. Source: http://198.1.102.91/talks/tedxteen-2013/163-maria-toorpakai-wazir-squashing-extremism

FEMALE FIRSTS IN SPORTS

1900: MARGARET ABBOTT wins a gold medal in golf; she is the first American woman to win at an Olympic event.

1920: ETHELDA BLEIBTREY becomes the first woman to win gold in swimming. She wins three! To this day, she remains the only woman to win all the swimming events in one year of the Olympic Games.

1926: New York City native **GERTRUDE EDERLE** becomes the first woman to swim the English Channel, swimming the thirty-five miles in fourteen hours and thirty-one minutes.

1949: SARA CHRISTIAN becomes the first female NASCAR driver.

1950: KATHRYN JOHNSTON cuts off her braids and dresses as a boy to attend baseball tryouts. She makes the team, becoming the first girl to play Little League Baseball.

1951: BETTY CHAPMAN is the first African American professional softball player. She plays as an outfielder.

1975: Japanese mountaineer **JUNKO TABEI** climbs Mount Everest—the first woman to do so.

1988: JACKIE JOYNER-KERSEE wins gold in the heptathlon. She also becomes the first American woman to win gold in the long jump.

2016: IBITIHAJ MUHAMMAD becomes the first U.S. Olympian to compete in the Rio Olympic Games while dressed in a hijab.